Original title:
Echoes of the Elder Forest

Copyright © 2025 Creative Arts Management OÜ
All rights reserved.

Author: Sebastian Whitmore
ISBN HARDBACK: 978-1-80567-414-6
ISBN PAPERBACK: 978-1-80567-713-0

Forest Shrouded in Mystery

In the woods where trees wear hats,
Chattering squirrels tell tall chats.
Mushrooms sport a polka dot show,
While owls hoot jokes that only they know.

The brook babbles with a bubbly laugh,
As deer trip over the silly giraffe.
Frogs stage plays with their croaky songs,
All the while, the wind hums along.

Chronicles of the Twilight Woods

In the twilight, shadows play hide and seek,
Where bunnies hop and the crickets speak.
A raccoon with a mask tells ghost tales,
While fairies dance on shimmering trails.

Old trees whisper secrets from long ago,
But all the squirrels just want to throw.
A clever fox with a laugh so sly,
Winks at the moon as it floats by.

Murmurs of Eternity in the Pines

The pines gossip softly, a ticklish breeze,
While chipmunks tease, stealing nuts with ease.
A wise old turtle gives advice so grand,
On how to build castles out of sand.

With acorns as currency, they trade and jest,
While playful raccoons put luck to the test.
The sun dips low as the night brings cheer,
With shadows that sway, dancing near.

The Ageless Dance of the Green Canopy

In the canopy green, the leaves do twist,
As squirrels partake in a nutty tryst.
Dance parties happen among the boughs,
With owls spinning in their feathered vows.

The forest floor booms with the rhythm of paws,
As rabbits cheer on with the loudest applause.
It's a waltz of whimsy, a festival bright,
In a place where the critters party all night.

Symphony of the Silent Sentinels

In the woods, the trees conspire,
Birds practicing band, all in wire.
Squirrels dance on the branch so high,
Chasing each other, oh my, oh my!

Bacon-scented winds swirl around,
While owls hoot in a puzzled sound.
A raccoon strums on a guitar,
Crowds gather to cheer, 'You're a star!'

Reflections in the Leafy Mirror

The pond sparkles with fishy grins,
As frogs croak tunes that nobody wins.
A turtle forgot where he left his hat,
While a busy ant declares, 'I'm just too fat!'

Leaves giggle as they dance in the breeze,
Tickling tree trunks, making them sneeze.
A playful breeze knows all the jokes,
Rustling whispers, while everyone pokes.

Journey Through Age-Old Trails

Fungi have formed a quirky club,
Mushrooms grinning as they thud.
A fox says, 'I am the wise old sage!'
While raccoons steal snacks from the age-old page.

Walking paths, so twisty and fun,
Where shadows dance, and races are run.
A lost rabbit, reading the map,
Turns in circles with a confused clap.

Legends of the Whispering Woods

A legend tells of a horned goat,
Whose bleat could make the bravest float.
Moths wear togas, as night airs in,
While owls share stories of a pie-eating win.

The trees gossip under starlit skies,
With woeful tales and questionable lies.
'Who stole my acorns?' a squirrel laments,
While everyone's laughing at the nonsense.

Pathways to Whispering Dreams

In the woods where gnomes roam free,
Squirrels chuckle from the tree.
With acorns tossed like tiny bombs,
A raccoon dances, oh so calm.

Branches swaying, what a sight,
A rabbit prancing left and right.
Whispers float on breezy trails,
While owls share their secret tales.

As the Oaks Watch Over Us

Beneath the oaks so grand and tall,
The critters giggle, having a ball.
With nuts and berries in their stash,
A deer in slippers makes a splash.

A squirrel in shades, oh what a flair,
Playing tag without a care.
The mossy floor, a cozy bed,
Where snoring foxes dream instead.

The Solstice Dance of Roots and Leaves

When the sun dips low and shadows grow,
The forest parties, putting on a show.
Roots entwined, they twist and spin,
While frogs in tuxedos suddenly begin.

Fireflies frolic, lighting the night,
As badgers boast of their best flight.
With laughter echoing through the trees,
The night unfolds with giggles and wheeze.

Chronicles carved in Bark

Trees hold stories, etched with care,
Of raccoons' heists and stargazing bears.
Each knot and swirl tells a tale,
Of feathered friends and a squirrel's fail.

Mushrooms chuckle at whispered fun,
As the forest breathes, shadows run.
With quirky critters all around,
In this wild realm, joy is found.

Reflections in the Woodland Glade

In a glade where squirrels jive,
Mice wear hats, look so alive.
Frogs croak jokes that make us cheer,
Even birds laugh with a sneer.

A tree once tripped, fell on a log,
Claimed it danced, oh what a grog!
Mushrooms chuckled, rolling in glee,
"Next time, stick with the grass, please!"

The Heartbeat of the Enchanted Thicket

In thickets thick, where rabbits laugh,
A hedgehog juggles, doing math.
Trees sway gently, dance with glee,
Even the rocks hum a melody.

The foxes hold a witty debate,
On how to dance without a plate.
Owls make takeout, quite a spread,
Whispering secrets of the dead.

Rustling Tales from the Deep Canopy

Leaves rustle, hear them sing,
Chattering critters, a lively fling.
A beaver with dreams of a tall tower,
Says, "I can build in just an hour!"

The raccoons play cards by the stream,
Cheating their friends, oh what a scheme!
The owls hoot 'til late in the night,
Bets piled high like a grand old sight.

Nature's Choir of Forgotten Seasons

Seasons talk, in quirky tones,
Winter wears socks made of bones.
Spring jumps in with a flower parade,
Daisies giggle, don't be afraid!

Summer sways in a bright yellow hat,
Drawing doodles, with a chat.
Fall joins in with a leafy grin,
Rolling pumpkins down, oh what a win!

Whispers Beneath the Canopy

In the forest, squirrels chatter,
Belly laughs, they tease and flatter.
Rabbits hop, doing silly spins,
While owls hoot, counting their sins.

Mice wear hats made out of leaves,
Dancing round with the rustling heaves.
Bears in bow ties join the fun,
Giggling hard, oh what a run!

Shadows and Secrets of Ancient Woods

Hiding under roots, a fox makes a plan,
To start a band with a toothy old man.
The raccoon plays drums with a coconut shell,
While the hedgehog performs, oh, can't you tell?

In the twilight, all creatures gather,
To share their jokes, it's a wild clatter.
The porcupine juggles berries with glee,
As laughter spills out, wild and free!

The Song of Timeworn Trees

Old trees sway, their branches hum,
With stories of critters, oh so fun!
The woodpecker's beat brings forth a tune,
That even the bugs tap dance to, soon.

The lizard strums on a twig for flair,
With a flair for comedy, beyond compare.
While the ants form a chorus, loud and bright,
Singing of mischief into the night.

Reverberations Among the Ancient Boughs

The tall pines gossip, with tops in a whirl,
Spreading news of the chipmunk's twirl.
Breezes carry giggles, through branches they sway,
As the sun sets low, ending their play.

The breeze whispers secrets, a tickle of air,
The frogs leap, croaking, without a care.
All gather round for the campfire's glow,
Sharing their tales, as the laughter flows.

Resonance of the Rooted Realm

In a grove where squirrels chatter,
A fox wore boots, oh, what's the matter?
A raccoon juggles acorns with flair,
While the owls debate in their easy chair.

The trees gossip about the shy fawn,
Who dances at dawn on the dew-kissed lawn.
A chipmunk sings in a voice quite high,
As the glimmering fireflies zip on by.

Ballad of the Twilight Thickets

Amidst the thickets, grasshoppers sing,
A turtle wears glasses, what a funny thing!
Beneath the moon's glow, the hedgehogs prance,
While the nightingale leads the woodland dance.

The porcupine's hairdo is quite the sight,
He claims he's a rock star every moonlit night.
A clumsy badger trips over his snack,
But laughs with joy, there's no skill to lack.

The Pulse of Nature's Heart

The bees buzz softly, plotting some games,
While the wise old owl rolls his eyes at their claims.
A family of worms holds a wiggly race,
And the leaves cheer on with a rustling grace.

The ferns all giggle at acorns' high dive,
As the brook splashes laughter, oh, how it thrives!
With a flick of his tail, a fish gives a wink,
Nature's delight makes us stop and think.

Sages of the Sylvan Shadows

The squirrels hold council on branches so high,
Debating which nut is the best for the pie.
A wise old crow tells tales of the past,
As the little grey mice listen, eyes wide and fast.

A hedgehog with glasses reads tales without sound,
While crickets chirp loudly, they really astound.
In the shadows of twilight, fun echoes around,
With laughter of nature, a joy profound.

The Unraveling Tale of the Woodland Dusk.

Once a squirrel wore a hat,
He thought it quite a feat.
But winds blew strong with a thud,
And sent him off his feet!

The owl hooted in delight,
As branches danced around.
The hat flew up into the night,
And made a tree-nest sound!

A sloth rolled by, so slow,
With leaves stuck to his back.
He offered snacks to all below,
While still on his lazy track.

And should you hear a laugh at dusk,
From creatures big and small,
Just know they've shed their serious husk,
In that enchanted hall!

Whispers in the Canopy

A parrot sang like a rock star,
With lyrics oh so wild.
But other birds thought it bizarre,
And labeled him their child.

The branches swayed in a jig,
As critters joined the song.
Even a snail danced a gig,
Though joining took too long!

Beneath, the rabbits tapped their feet,
To a rhythm made of twigs.
The trees swirled like they had heat,
While squirrels did silly digs.

As night fell, laughter spread,
From root to lofty peak.
A secret dance that found its thread,
In whispers soft and cheek!

Shadows of Ancient Giants

Old trees tell tales of yore,
In shadows, thick and wide.
They chuckle at the forest floor,
Where tiny creatures hide.

A beaver wore a monocle,
And surveyed the flowing stream.
His friends thought it comical,
A fashion statement dream!

While near a stump, a raccoon pranced,
With berries on his hat.
He led a dance, all were entranced,
Including a surprised cat.

As dusk set in, the fun grew strong,
In the heart of tangled roots.
The ancient ones rocked along,
In forest's silly suits!

Voices Beneath the Verdant Veil

In leafy dens, the gnomes conspire,
With jokes that make you grin.
They trade tall tales and never tire,
As daylight wears thin.

A badger tried to play the flute,
But sounded more like yowls.
His friends joined in, oh what a hoot,
The night turned into howls!

The ferns swayed to their giggle spree,
As fireflies lit the way.
A chorus loud, as wild as can be,
Brought magic to the day.

So if you hear a joyous roar,
From clusters green and bright,
Know it's the woodland, evermore,
Up to funny, frolicsome delight!

The Language of Ancient Leaves

In the treetops, secrets swayed,
Leaves converse in a light parade.
One claims the sun, another shade,
While squirrels dance in woodland charade.

Whispers shared on a gentle breeze,
Rustling tales of ancient trees.
"Hey, I'm older!" one leaf teases,
Suddenly, all fall down like sneezes.

Mossy knights in armor sprout,
Guarding stories we laugh about.
Barking trees must have their doubts,
As the forest giggles and shouts.

Guardians of the Good Green

Watch the gnomes with their silly hats,
Chasing rabbits, dodging bats.
In a world where mischief be—
They trip on roots, and oh, woe is me!

Frogs in tuxedos croak and boast,
"Who hops better?" they argue most.
But one with flair wins the race,
While others leap at a slower pace.

A wise old owl starts to snore,
As raccoons plan a late-night score.
"Steal the snacks but hide the crumbs!"
To the forest's rhythm, laughter hums.

Secrets of the Swaying Branches

Branches whisper, snicker, sway,
As they plot a playful foray.
"Let's tickle the crow!" says one twig,
As giggles bounce with every dig.

Once a squirrel tried to spill,
A stash of acorns, what a thrill!
They rolled and rolled, like tiny stars,
Causing chaos from afar.

Each rustle carries jokes galore,
With hidden treasures, and then some more.
Nature's jesters, they weave and twine,
In their leafy realm, oh how they shine!

A Melodic Murmur of the Mindful Wood

Listen close to the forest's tune,
Frolicking fawns and an old raccoon.
They dance and prance with light hearts,
Making music as nature imparts.

Bees buzz a rhythm, cicadas sing,
While wiggly worms do their spring fling.
A grand waltz spun in sunlit streams,
Tickles of laughter in woodland dreams.

The brook giggles, the shadows sway,
As twilight winks at the end of day.
So join this jolly woodland spree,
In the light-hearted melody of glee.

Chronicles of the Rooted Ancients

In the shadow, a squirrel did prance,
With a nut in hand, he took a chance.
He told a tale, dramatic and bold,
Of the acorns saved, treasures of old.

A wise old owl, perched on a limb,
Chimed in laughter, his eyes a-glimmer.
"Tell me more, you cheeky old nut,
What's your secret? Do you hide in the hut?"

The squirrel replied with a wink and a grin,
"It's the secret of stash, now let's begin!"
And so, they plotted, a forest heist,
To gather the acorns, oh what a feast!

But roots got tangled in the merry scuffle,
The owl hooted loud, oh what a shuffle!
"Next time we'll plan on a map, my friend,
Let's not get wrapped in the forest's bend!"

The Gentle Gaze of the Glade

In the glade, where the butterflies play,
A rabbit danced in a rather odd way.
With hopping and flopping, he joined the song,
While frogs croaked the chorus, all night long.

A turtle, slow and steady, stood near,
He claimed he'd win the hopping premiere.
"I may be sluggish, but I've got the charm,
Just watch me glide, causing no alarm!"

The rabbit turned, chuckling with glee,
"That'll be the day! You can't catch me!"
Yet, underneath the moon's silver stare,
The turtle won races, with grace rare.

So if you wander, with laughter as kin,
Remember the lesson tucked in the din:
Sometimes the slow and steady are great,
And prancing doesn't always navigate fate!

The Song of the Silent Pines

Amidst the pines, a songbird squawked,
He perched on a branch, his antics unlocked.
He sang of a hawk with an oversized hat,
That thought he was cool but just looked like that!

The pines began swaying, like they understood,
Joining the laughter, they swayed very good.
Each gust of wind was a giggle so sly,
As pine needles whispered, "Oh my, oh my!"

Then came a deer, with antlers askew,
She laughed at the hawk; that was nothing new.
"We'll wear our own hats, so let's make a stand,
With pine cones and yes, a soft leafy band!"

So pines kept swaying, and the bird did sing,
A concert of jest, oh what joy they bring!
Adventures in style, with laughter in tow,
Nature's own delight, putting on a show!

Stories Wrapped in Vines

In a tangle of green, the vines made a fuss,
A raccoon recounted a tale just for us.
He spoke of a picnic, food all around,
Until a bear waltzed in, no peace to be found.

The vines wrapped tighter, as laughter took flight,
"That bear was so hungry, he ate till the night!"
They giggled and jiggled at the thought of his feast,
Imagining sandwiches, fried chicken, and yeast.

"And what of the ants?" questioned a vine,
"Did they join the party, or stayed behind?"
The raccoon just chuckled, "Oh, they marched right through,
Claiming their share, a whole line of the crew!"

So tales intertwined, within the vine's embrace,
Of raccoons and bears, in this whimsical space.
If you listen quite closely, you'll find they're divine,
All stories in laughter, wrapped up in the vine!

Ballads from the Bark

In the trees, the squirrels dance,
Chasing shadows, not a chance.
Birch leaves whisper with delight,
As raccoons steal the moonlit night.

Old oak grumbles, 'Where's my drink?'
Sippy cups, they make him think.
Woodpeckers tap, a funny beat,
Dancing bugs beneath their feet.

Mossy mats, a comfy bed,
Frogs croak jokes that must be read.
Lizards laugh in the warm sun,
Nature's crew just having fun.

Nuts and acorns thrown in play,
Squirrels munch their blues away.
Branches sway with giggles clear,
In this wood, the joy is near.

Secrets of the Ancient Twilight

In twilight woods, the shadows grow,
Where secrets of the past will flow.
A fox in glasses reads a tome,
While owls share stories from their home.

Gnomes in flannel, sipping tea,
Planning mischief, oh so free.
Toadstools giggle, mushrooms sway,
They know how to enjoy the day.

The breeze brings laughter through the leaves,
As each tree wears its old sleeves.
Raccoons with masks, a bandit crew,
Stealing snacks, 'Oh, who knew?'

Yet, in this twilight, wisdom gleams,
The forest holds its silly dreams.
With every chuckle, every jest,
Nature's humor, simply the best.

Echoes of the Verdant Depths

In deepest greens where shadows dance,
Old roots whisper, 'Take a chance!'
A beetle dons a shiny hat,
While tiny crickets play a rat.

Leaves gossip in the warming light,
Sharing tales of quirky sight.
The hedgehog rolls, a naked ball,
And shows the world he's quite the stall.

Beavers build with logs and cheer,
Chopping wood, they have no fear.
Chipmunks juggle 'neath the stars,
While fireflies twinkle near the spar.

In verdant depths, fun reigns supreme,
As laughter echoes like a dream.
The forest thrives in silly ways,
Reminding us to enjoy our days.

Tales Woven in Wood

Whispers woven through the bark,
As night falls in the little park.
A raccoon tells a joke or two,
While owls review their old menu.

Woodpeckers laugh at tree trunk pranks,
Silly dance among the ranks.
The picnic ants begin to sing,
Dreaming of a food-filled spring.

Squirrels plot with a furrowed brow,
How to steal a nut from now.
Leaves dance along a breezy flow,
In their world, it's all a show.

Tales of wood, both caught and spun,
Nature's theater, lots of fun.
From roots to branches, joy takes flight,
In the wood's embrace, all feels right.

Votes of the Venerable Woods

Tall trees gather, mutter low,
Branches sway in whimsical flow.
"Who gets the crown?" the squirrels debate,
While mushrooms giggle at their fate.

Acorns drop like ballots cast,
With every plop, their fun amassed.
The winds all whisper, 'What a scene!'
As bark-clad judges look quite keen.

The rabbits hop around with glee,
Counting nuts beneath the leafy spree.
A fox in glasses takes the lead,
While badgers grumble, 'This is greed!'

In the tall grass, a hedgehog snores,
Dreaming of victories and open doors.
Yet all agree, at day's fun end,
Only the ticks are left to spend.

The Narrative of Nature

In the throng of twigs and bloom,
Nature's tales dance in the room.
A snail, a bard, tells tales so grand,
While ants take notes, a tiny band.

The winds play tricks, a gusty tease,
Whispering secrets to the trees.
While wise old owls hoot with cheek,
Debating dreams while they sneak a peek.

The sunbeams laugh, their warmth a jest,
As shadows stretch, they'll never rest.
The streams recite their bubbling rhyme,
While frogs debate the silliest mime.

A butterfly slips through the crowd,
Announcing loudly, "I'm quite proud!"
With nature's mischief all around,
It's laughter ringing, joy unbound.

The Forest's Gentle Echo

In the glade where critters play,
Soft chuckles float on breezy sway.
Squirrels slip, then tripping fall,
And then they laugh, the trees stand tall.

A bear named Lou, with honey grins,
Wants to dance, despite his sins.
"Two left feet!" the dancers squeal,
As he cascades like a rolling wheel.

The owls hoot, with wise old cheer,
"Who knew this wood could bring such jeer?"
But every step brings smiles anew,
As life unfolds with joy's own brew.

When night descends, and starlight's cast,
The woodland whirls, its shadows vast.
Each creature giggles, finds their friend,
In this light-hearted dance that'll never end.

Breaths of the Woodland's Heart

Amid the trees, where smiles grow,
Nature ponders the silliest show.
A weasel juggles, oh what a sight,
While birds chirp jokes in sheer delight.

Frogs wear hats, with tails that twist,
In this woodland scene, how can you resist?
Each flower giggles, swaying in tune,
Under the glow of a cheeky moon.

The bumblebees turn into clowns,
Buzzing around with silly gowns.
A hedgehog prances, searching for fun,
Joining the laughs until the day is done.

In this world of laughter's embrace,
Every creature finds its place.
So let us frolic, nature's cheer,
In this vibrant heart, we hold so dear.

Secrets of the Timeworn Grove

In a grove where the old trees stand,
Squirrels debate with a nut in hand.
They chatter away as they leap and bound,
While mushrooms giggle, spread out on the ground.

A raccoon plots to steal a snack,
But the wise old owl sees through his act.
He hoots with laughter, keeps watch from above,
As critters below share a tale wrapped in love.

Beneath the bark, a wise beetle grins,
As the tree trunk shakes with tickles and spins.
Each branch and leaf knows the humor abound,
In the secrets whispered all around.

With shadows dancing, the night takes flight,
Glowworms twinkle, offering light.
What a party! The woods come alive,
Where laughter grows and dreams can thrive.

Reverberations of the Green

In the heart of the woods, where the green grass sways,
Frogs croak out ballads with humorous ways.
They sing to the stars with a croaky delight,
As fireflies join in, winking their light.

A hedgehog rolls by, in a spin that won't stop,
Trying to escape from a playful raindrop.
He chuckles and tumbles, a ball of good cheer,
While the rabbits all cheer for their brave little peer.

Trees shake their leaves, sharing jokes of the past,
With wisdom that echoes, surprises that last.
Each creature joins in on this woodland spree,
What fun we have in our party of three!

As night falls softly, and shadows commence,
The giggles and murmurs start growing immense.
With a hilltop of laughter and joy that won't cease,
The grand green reverberates, a giggly peace.

The Oldest Trees Sing

The oldest trees lean close and sway,
Sharing stories in the funniest way.
A parrot joins in, sings out of tune,
While critters below hum a merry cartoon.

With twisted branches, they crack little jokes,
While coyotes yip loud, joining in pokes.
"Why did the crow wear a fancy new hat?"
"To look quite dapper while sitting on that!"

The moss-covered stumps echo giggles galore,
As the badger rolls on the forest floor.
In the twilight glow, all the laughter grows,
Around trunks and boughs, mischief overflows.

Old owls give winks, sharing wisdom they glean,
In this funny forest, awash in the green.
With voices in chorus, vibrant and bold,
The roots of the grove share secrets untold.

Murmurs of the Woodland Spirits

In the depths where the whispers twirl,
Woodland spirits giggle, and leaves uncurl.
They dance 'round the trunks with delight and flair,
As the squirrels jump high, floating in air.

Each rustle and laugh brings a sparkle of fun,
Where mushrooms recite as the day is done.
"Why was the tree always happy and grand?
Because it had branches and lots of good friends!"

As twilight descends, they hide and seek,
The shadows grow longer, a playful peek.
"Catch me if you can!" they jovially sing,
With the chirps of crickets, life's grandest fling.

In our grove of secrets, where humor aligns,
The woodland spirits weave laughter in lines.
With every soft murmur, they thrive and sway,
In a world filled with joy, where mischief holds sway.

The Tapestry of the Time-Worn Trails

In the woods where old trees tell,
Squirrels dance, oh what the smell!
Fungi giggle, hiding from sight,
While raccoons toss leaves, full of delight.

Branches wave like hands in cheer,
As the chipmunks start to leer.
A wise old owl drops a pun,
"Why was the pine tree always fun?"

"Because it knew how to have a bough!"
He hoots, and all the critters bow.
Laughter rings as shadows blend,
In this jungle, joy won't end.

With every turn, a twist unfolds,
Nature's jests, forever bold.
So skip along and voice your glee,
In this grand wood, wild and free.

Nature's Hidden Histories

In the bark of ancient trees,
Lie tales of bees and buzzing frees.
A beetle tells of winters past,
While mushrooms giggle, growing fast.

Each root a story, each leaf a laugh,
Lizards posing, they love to quaff.
A snail claims it moves at great speed,
"Just give me time, I'll take the lead!"

The brook hums tunes of silly tunes,
As frogs forget their moonlit croons.
Squirrels snicker at the funny sights,
Chasing shadows, what a night!

With whispers blowing through green glades,
The humor thrives in dappled shades.
So lean in close and lend an ear,
Nature's punchlines are always near.

The Night's Ballad Beneath the Stars

Beneath the stars, a deer holds court,
Telling tales, a lively sport.
The moon rolls in with a wink and grin,
As fireflies flash their sparks within.

A raccoon sings about his feast,
"No fish tonight—just bread and yeast!"
The owls hoot with a wise old tune,
While the crickets tap dance, under the moon.

The night is alive with chuckles and cheers,
As shadows cast away all fears.
Each rustle in the brush brings delight,
In the playful antics of the night.

So gather 'round for nature's show,
Where laughter flows and good times grow.
With starlit skies and a heart so warm,
In nature's arms, we find our charm.

The Wisdom of the Weathered Bark

The trees stand tall with tales of yore,
Their bark adorned with wisdom galore.
"Knock knock! Who's there?" a squirrel starts,
A giggle blossoms in nature's arts.

Old pines whisper of winds that blew,
While laughing leaves dance, tipping dew.
"I'm not old, just a seasoned pro!"
The branches sway, putting on a show.

Woodpeckers tap with a rhythmic beat,
As rabbits share snacks, quite a treat.
"What do you call a tree that knows?"
The ancient oak, its laughter grows.

"A wise old limb, that's who!" it says,
And all around it, the forest plays.
So heed the joy in the trunk's embrace,
For humor thrives in this green space.

Lullabies from a Thousand Branches

In the trees where critters chat,
Squirrels sing and birds tip their hat.
A sleepy owl rolls its big eyes,
Sways to the wind, what a surprise!

Beneath the boughs, the raccoons dance,
Trying hard not to lose their pants.
Giggles burst from the thicket's hide,
Nature's jest unfolds with pride.

The badger croons a funny tune,
While mice draw near by the light of moon.
A visit from the hedgehog crew,
Bouncing and laughing, who knew?

With every chuckle, nuts will fall,
A merry feast for one and all.
In this place where laughter's free,
The forest whispers joyfully!

The Wisdom of the Worn Pathways

Upon the trail, where footsteps land,
The wise old trees make their stand.
They giggle softly, roots entwined,
    At all the silliness they find.

A turtle wearing clogs stumbles by,
While a tall grasshopper tries to fly.
The path knows tales of every fall,
Like the bird who mistook a wall!

As wanderers trip and tumble down,
The ferns just rustle, don't wear a frown.
With leaves that whisper, 'Stay the course,'
    The wind adds wit, a merry force.

So heed the ground that's been well-trod,
    It holds the laughter of each odd.
With stories woven through the air,
    The journey's joy is everywhere!

Fenland Memories by Moonlight

In the fen where the frogs hold court,
They play the games of wild retort.
A firefly leads a dance so bright,
While shadows laugh under the moonlight.

Swans in tuxedos float with flair,
Winking at fishes without a care.
A turtle in a top hat takes a stroll,
Joking about losing his shoelace goal.

Crickets conspire with mischievous glee,
As the reeds weave tales of jubilee.
"Hop on, it's a ribbiting ride!"
With misty laughter, they seem so spry.

The moon confides with a cheeky grin,
"Life's a laugh, let the fun begin!"
In this wetland mirth and song,
Nights like this can't be wrong!

Lost in the Timbered Reverie

Amidst the woods, where shadows play,
The chipmunks plot a nutty ballet.
With twirls and spins, they're full of flair,
"Who needs a stage? We own the air!"

A raccoon dons a mask of style,
Winks as he dances, "Just watch my smile!"
Trees giggle softly, swaying to beat,
As nature throws an evening treat.

With every bounce and cheeky cheer,
The woodland wonders draw us near.
"We're all a bit nuts, don't you see?
Join the fun, just let it be!"

So when lost in laughter, take a chance,
Dance with the trees in a whimsical trance.
For in the woods, where all is free,
The best of frivolity's the key!

The Soliloquy of the Old Growth

In the woods where the trees stand tall,
Squirrels debate, "Who'll win the fall?"
Barking at trunks, they shout with glee,
"Forget the acorns, let's climb the tree!"

Mossy gents with wisdom so deep,
Whisper secrets while others sleep.
They boast of times when they were young,
Now they stretch, leaves getting hung!

The owls roll eyes at the youthful game,
"Back in my day, we had more fame!"
They chuckle softly, wings not in strife,
While trees share tales of a longer life.

So gather round, let us toast, my friends,
To the whacky wisdom that never ends!
In this hallowed stage, where laughs take flight,
Nature's punchlines make everything right.

Twilight Conversations in the Arboreal Realm

As dusk drapes the leaves in dress so fine,
Crickets chirp a weird little line.
"Is it too late for a moonlit dance?"
"Only if tripping's part of the chance!"

Leaves gossip softly, their stories unfold,
About the acorns, all riches untold.
"Did you see that owl with its clumsy swoop?"
"Totally crashed — what a funny loop!"

The fireflies flicker, holding a glow,
"Let's start a rave, just listen to flow!"
Laughter resumes beneath the dark sky,
While shadows do twists and turns nearby.

With giggles and snorts, the woods come alive,
Creatures of night in an uproar dive.
Under the stars, they play hide and seek,
In this grand ballroom, they laugh and peek!

Fables of the Sylvan Shadows

Woodland tales with a twist of jest,
Dandelions dream of being the best.
"Flowers should sing!" shouts an old weed,
"But who has the voice, we all concede!"

The spruce, with its wispy branches so spry,
Tells muffled stories as time goes by.
"Remember that time the rabbit wore socks?
He raced with the turtle, dodged clever blocks!"

Among tangled roots, mischief resides,
A parade of ants with snack time collides.
"More crumbs, less grumbles!" the queen's royal cry,
As a curious hedgehog wobbles on by.

So gather your tales, let's share them around,
In these wooded halls, laughter is found.
A tapestry woven with giggles and lore,
In the vibrant shadows, life's never a bore.

The Unspoken Bond of the Forest Floor

Under the canopy, whispers so light,
Mushrooms dance under the moon's soft light.
"Who said fungi can't put on a show?"
With a top hat and cape, they steal the show!

Rabbits with wigs hold an elegant feast,
"Let's munch on greens, not on the beast!"
With carrots arranged as their fancy buffet,
They laugh at a fox who's lost on the way.

A chipmunk recounts a great misadventure,
"Chased by a dog, I found my indenture!"
The laughter erupts, leaves start to sway,
Nature's own comedy, in a leafy ballet.

In the depths of the woods where dreams intertwine,
A party erupts, all creatures align.
With each little giggle, the night carries on,
Celebrating life till the break of dawn!

Beneath the Shroud of Leaves

Beneath the green, the squirrels play,
Chasing shadows, day by day.
A chipmunk's dance, a jester's twirl,
Who knew the woods could host such a whirl?

With acorns launched like tiny bombs,
In comedic skirmishes, nature calms.
A rabbit's hop, a deer's quick look,
All trapped within this greenish nook.

The owls hoot in bemused delight,
Watching antics through the night.
While raccoons plot their next big heist,
In this forest, laughter's spiced.

So tiptoe through the leafy maze,
And don't forget to laugh for days.
For nature's humor is ever true,
With funny friends and sights anew.

Reflections Among the Timeless Trees

A frog sings operas from a log,
While beetles mingle, dressed in fog.
A chorus of critters, pure delight,
Their tiny tales, a joyful sight.

A deer trips over roots too proud,
Stumbles, then bows before the crowd.
With giggles shared, the forest glows,
Life's silly moments, how it flows.

Pixies play with dandelion seeds,
Creating wishes that sprout like weeds.
While trees chuckle at the jest,
In this fairground, nature's best.

The brook gurgles a teasing rhyme,
As the sun sets, it's punchline time.
So gather round, let laughter swell,
In a world of wonder, all is well.

The Shadows Hold Many Stories

In the dark, where shadows blend,
A raccoon plans a prank, my friend.
With a flick of the tail, and a wink of the eye,
"Can you believe it?" the owls reply.

The trees whisper funny secrets, too,
"Did you hear about the fox that lost his shoe?"
With rustling leaves, they cackle and sway,
As the moonlight joins the nightly play.

Badgers roll in soft, wet mud,
Thinking it's a spa—oh, what a dud!
While the night critters share their laughs,
The wise old owl, in knowing halves.

So come, share tales where shadows dance,
For amongst the gloom, there's always a chance.
To find in the dark, a glittering glee,
As laughter echoes among the trees.

Songs of the Boughs at Dusk

As dusk descends, the branches sway,
With twinkling stars that join the play.
A woodpecker's tap, a rhythm so bright,
Encourages critters to join in the flight.

A squirrel holds a concert, grand and bold,
With acorns for drums, and tales retold.
Chipmunks harmonize, a cheeky choir,
Under moonlight's glow, they never tire.

Hares hop along, keeping time with glee,
Dancing through the night, wild and free.
"Not too fast!" squeaks a mouse, quite wise,
"Or we'll trip over fireflies!"

So sing with me, 'neath the boughs so high,
Where laughter rings and worries fly.
For in the soft glow of fading light,
The forest hums its tunes so bright.

Sylvan Memories in the Mist

In the woodlands where critters creep,
Squirrels plot and giggle, no time for sleep.
Rabbits wear hats made of leaves and twine,
Throwing dance parties, it's simply divine.

A bear in a tutu does twirls and spins,
While hedgehogs in bowties play games with chins.
The trees play a tune with a rustling glee,
As raccoons serve punch from an old teapot spree.

Mice like to skateboard on stumps made of oak,
Each trick gets applause, it's no mere joke.
With mushrooms as bleachers and ferns as the stage,
The woodland gets rowdy, full of playful rage.

So if you should wander where magic takes flight,
Join in on the fun, we party 'til night.
With laughter and mischief, the woods come alive,
These memories linger, here spirits will thrive.

Murmurs of the Forgotten Grove

In a grove where the shadows play hide and seek,
A babbling brook sings tunes, never meek.
Raccoons slip in, trying to dive,
How they can tumble! Oh, they'd never survive.

An owl on a branch tries to know all the jokes,
But even wise ones get tangled with pokes.
"Who's there?" he hoots with a grin on his face,
While frogs hop around, sending laughter through space.

The foxes debate on who's fastest in town,
With bets made in acorns, a true woodland crown.
Each trickster a champion, a laughable mess,
As creatures unite for this cheerful contest.

So join in the chatter beneath leafy cheer,
Where every sweet murmur brings joy to the ear.
The forgotten will dance, the past made to gleam,
In this silly ol' grove, where nothing's as it seems.

Chronicles of the Woodland Spirits

In the heart of the forest, where whispers abound,
Silly spirits frolic, twirling 'round.
A pixie named Crafty, with yarn in her hands,
Stitches together delightful green strands.

A gnome with a wink welcomes all with a grin,
His potions bring giggles, oh what a win!
"Try this one, my friend, it's fizzy and bright!"
As the moonlight bursts forth, it's pure delight.

The owls hoot rhymes full of twinkling delight,
While squirrels recite tales of their late-night flight.
Each branch holds a secret, wrapped up in a laugh,
As creatures unite for a whimsical path.

So wander with wonder, let laughter erupt,
In this wood where the spirits have joyfully jumped.
Their chronicles dance like leaves in the breeze,
Forever enchanted, we'll hold onto these.

Secrets Held by the Gnarled Roots

Beneath the old oaks, where roots twist and twine,
Lies a party of gnomes sipping on pine.
They bounce on the soil, in mud-slinging games,
Where laughter erupts, and everyone claims.

A chipmunk plays trumpet, a bird strums the strings,
They bring forth a tune that just tickles and swings.
With mushrooms as drums and a snail as the beat,
There's jigging and jiving right over your seat.

In the knots of the trees, wise secrets are told,
Of mischief and mayhem, both daring and bold.
"Who stole my acorns?" a squirrel cries loud,
While laughter erupts from the woodland crowd.

So trust in these roots, let your spirit unwind,
For secrets they hold are silly and kind.
In this hidden nook where the playful convene,
A world full of joy, like you've never seen!

The Heart's Calling from Within the Woods

In a tree, a squirrel does dance,
Chasing shadows in a trance.
Otters giggle near the creek,
As raccoons plot their heist unique.

The owls hoot with a cheeky grin,
Gossiping about the latest sin.
Bears sipping tea, wearing hats,
Debating why squirrels have such spats.

The moonlight tickles the mossy ground,
While frogs join in with silly sounds.
A deer checks her makeup before the show,
As fireflies flash their patterns aglow.

In nature's theater, laughter reigns,
A chorus of critters knows no chains.
The heart beats louder with every joke,
As the woods burst forth with mirthful oak.

Spirits Whispering in the Breeze

Gentle sways of branches sway,
Marshmallows float in a leaf buffet.
Chirping crickets join the fun,
While the sun sets, the day's almost done.

A gopher juggles acorns with flair,
While beavers dance without a care.
Mice in capes hold a grand debate,
Over who makes the best cheese plate.

The wind plays tunes that tickle the trees,
Like a band of sprites, all buzzing with ease.
A shy fox blushes, turns the wrong way,
As the moonlight giggles, "Oh, what a play!"

Through whispers of leaves, laughter is found,
In every rustle, joy resounds.
A meeting of spirits both silly and free,
In a woodland bar, sipping honeyed tea.

The Leafy Library of Tales

Books made of bark piled up high,
In a nook where the wise owls fly.
Bunnies read drama by firelight,
While hedgehogs tell tales of a cheeky fight.

A porcupine pens a love letter,
To a badger, who thinks he's a trendsetter.
The plot thickens with every page,
As skunks take stage with stinky rage.

Squirrels juggling walnuts, oh what a sight,
While moles narrate history late at night.
A chorus of tales fills the cool air,
From wild adventures to odd prairies rare.

Underneath stars, laughter erupts,
As every creature fully corrupts.
In this leafy library, deep and vast,
Every story echoes, its chortle cast.

The Quiet Counsel of the Cedars

Cedars stand tall with wisdom to share,
While raccoons plot with crafty flair.
A council of critters, serious and wise,
Discussing the latest in woodland ties.

Their serious chatter turns into a feast,
As a fox drops jokes like a friendly beast.
Chickadees chuckle at every pun,
While tree frogs leap, oh what fun!

A turtle offers sage advice,
"Slow down folks, take a slice!"
Goblins giggle in the tangled vines,
As moonshine drips in sparkling lines.

This council of laughter, life's workbird,
In the heart of the woods, where all are heard.
The whispers of wisdom float on the breeze,
As joy is shared beneath the trees.

The Heartbeat of the Olden Trees

In the shade of the ancient bark,
Squirrels plot their daring heist,
With acorns flown through the air,
Their treasure map's a bit too biased.

Branches dance like wobbly legs,
As wind plays pranks in a sunny glade,
The owls hoot jokes in the moonlight,
While mischievous fairies laugh and invade.

Rabbits hop with comic flair,
Tripping over roots in their way,
Each stumble turns into a tale,
That woodland critters share by day.

The trees thrum with laughter's beat,
As whispers weave through leafy spine,
In this quirky, leafy retreat,
Nature's comedy is just divine!

The Lore of the Timbered Heart

Once a tree told a joke to a bee,
"Why do you buzz like you're on a spree?"
The bee just chuckled, no time to waste,
Swirling around in a sweet, sticky haste.

A crow cawed tales on a sunny morn,
About how a pine was slightly worn,
He claimed it wore sneakers, not just bark,
And danced like a star in the dark.

The oaks conspired on who could best,
Appear older than the rest,
"We've seen more than just passing seasons,"
"Now let's compare our wilty reasons!"

Fallen branches lay low with pride,
As they reminisce with splits wide,
These timbered hearts share their fun,
In laughter that dances like the sun!

Nostalgia Beneath the Boughs

A memory drifts like a feathered kite,
Beneath the tall trees, a curious sight,
Where saplings blush at old, wise trunks,
And giggle as they trip on their hunks.

Rummaging critters scurry about,
Digging for nuts with a joyful shout,
Chasing their tails in the golden dust,
Even mushrooms seem to sprout with trust.

The breeze tells stories of youthful spright,
As shadows sway in the candlelight,
"Oh, the fun we had as a leafy crew!"
"Remember that time we grew all askew?"

A riddle posed by the old willow tree,
"Why's a squirrel better at climbing than me?"
The answer hangs on a tangled vine,
In laughter that twists like a vintage line!

Secrets of the Still Starlight

At night the trees hold a cabaret,
With crickets singing in a jazzy way,
The stars blink bright in a cheeky jest,
As owls sip tea, a royal fest.

Moonbeams dance on the leafy floor,
While raccoons plan for their late-night score,
"Got snacks?" one asked, in an earnest plea,
"Only if you share that honey with me!"

The night wind chuckles, rolling along,
Tickling the leaves with a playful song,
Whispers of mischief rustle and sway,
As darkness swathes the world in a play.

"Oh, hush!" the firs reply with a grin,
"We've secrets to keep from the day's din,
But under starlight, we'll laugh and spin,
In the still of the night, let the fun begin!"

Tales of the Forgotten Glade

In the shade where squirrels chatter,
Frogs jump high but always splatter.
Bunnies dance in a silly way,
While mushrooms giggle, 'Come, let's play!'

A hedgehog sneezes, starts a show,
As acorns tumble down below.
The owl hoots loud, 'Can you not see?
This forest's crazier than TV!'

Beneath the moss, a snail's on speed,
Chasing its friend, a slow-witted seed.
They laugh and roll, what a sight to see,
Who knew nature could be so zany?

But the trees just shake their leafy heads,
'Kids these days, all fun, no threads!'
Yet in their bark, they can't help but grin,
For laughter's a treasure that lies within.

Chronicles of the Timbered Titans

In a realm where tall trees hang low,
A squirrel maestro puts on a show.
He conducts the wind with frantic flair,
While butterflies dance without a care.

Among the giants, a snail sings blues,
Raccoons wear hats, while birds wear shoes.
The owls recite their poetry right,
As night sets in, igniting delight.

Beneath the boughs, a bear tells jokes,
As chipmunks snicker, sharing pokes.
The mushrooms laugh, with caps that sway,
While twilight whispers, 'End of the day!'

'What's faster than light?' asks a wise old bat,
'A raccoon in the night, now how about that?'
The trees just shimmy, roots tapping the ground,
For joy in the forest is always found.

The Lament of the Leafy Watchers

In the canopy, leaves wiggle and sway,
As they gossip about critters at play.
A rabbit hops, wearing a crown,
A sight so silly, they'd never frown.

There's a raccoon that thinks he's a star,
Dancing like he's in a far-off bazaar.
The whispers come from branches so wise,
Sharing secrets with cheeky sighs.

Down on the forest floor, ants are a team,
Carrying crumbs in a synchronized dream.
They plot a parade, uniforms bright,
While the trees croon softly, 'Oh what a sight!'

With a wiggle and jiggle, the leaves start to cheer,
For the forest is wild, with nothing to fear.
Even the shadows join in the fun,
Together they laugh until day is done.

Memories of Moss-Cloaked Paths

On paths where the sunlight likes to peek,
A tiny mouse plays hide and seek.
While a tortoise tells tales so grand,
Of cheese and kings in a faraway land.

A bee buzzes loudly, a comic relief,
As it tells of a flower that spread disbelief.
It claimed it was nectar, but flavor was bad,
Causing the butterflies to get quite mad!

Old toads on logs crack ancient puns,
About long-lost mushrooms and sprinting runs.
'Why did the chicken cross the stream?'
'To find a root that was living the dream!'

The paths are alive with laughter and jest,
As the creatures gather to share their best.
In this haven where mirth greets the day,
Who knew nature could be so cliché?

www.ingramcontent.com/pod-product-compliance
Lightning Source LLC
Chambersburg PA
CBHW072139200426
43209CB00051B/148